1

Right. I've got rid of the maid for an hour. I told her to bring me a pizza. She knows the sort I like but she'll get it wrong. Maria is Spanish and her English is not very good.

Now, where was I? I know. Get the video ready. Set up the camera. Take a seat. Look into the lens. Pretend it's a mate. Ready to record.

Click on

Call me Jack. Jack's just an ordinary name. I'm just an ordinary man. But last year I wasn't ordinary. Last year I think I was a bit crazy. And because I was crazy I got rich – very rich.

How come? I hear you ask. Did you win the pools? Did you get the lottery jackpot? Did someone die and leave you a fortune?

No, is the answer. I won nothing. No one ever left me a penny. My Mum died in a council flat ten years ago with an empty purse. Do you really want to hear how I got rich? I think you do. All right, I'll tell you. I stole a lot of money.

I know what you are thinking. How much? Have a guess. Go on. Was it a thousand? Ten thousand?

3

Have you given up? I'll tell you then. I stole two million . . . pounds, that is. That's real money where I come from, I don't know about you. It's not the sort of money you get from a kid's piggy-bank, is it?

I know what your next question is. How did he steal two million? Who has that sort of money? How did he get his hands on enough cash to last a lifetime?

I'll tell you. I stole it from a security van. I stole it when I was half crazy and now I'm living the sort of life you can only dream about. Here I am in sunny Spain – with a pool, a villa, and a maid called Maria to do all the work.

Want to hear how I did it? I'm going to tell you anyway. That's why I'm making this video. Don't go away . . .

Click off

I'll just check that it's all working. I'll run the video back and play the bit I've done so far. Now, let's see. How does it look? Picture – good. Sound – good. There I am in my living room. It's all in focus. You can even see the view out of my window. Yellow sand . . . blue sea . . . boats . . . people swimming.

It's all fine. I can carry on now.

2

Smile for the camera.

Click on

I always wanted to be rich. When I was a kid we were poor. My Dad died when I was a year old and Mum found it hard to bring up her four kids. I was the baby of the family. Little baby Jack.

There was no money for anything. I never got new clothes. I had to wear the stuff the other kids had grown out of. Mum worked all hours trying to make ends meet and the people she worked for treated her worse than the office cat.

I made a promise to myself. I promised that no one would put their boot on my neck. When I grew up I'd be rich. Then I would be the boss and I'd look after my dear old Mum in her old age.

But things didn't work out. I hated school and I used to skip classes. When I left I was out of work for a year. Then I got a few part-time jobs with next to no pay and no perks.

I worked in a store shifting carpets. I had to put them on a trolley and take them up to the sales floor. I saw posh people forking out more for a carpet than I got paid in a year. And what was I? I was a nobody.

I got bitter. I hated anyone I saw in a posh car. I used to think about my old Mum. I wanted to make something of myself – for her as much as for me. But how? I thought about it all day as I moved the carpets.

Then the boss called me in. He said, 'I'm sorry Jack, but you must go at the end of the week. You get oil from the trolley all over the carpets. You keep doing it. Your mind isn't on your work, Jack.'

So I got the sack. And then I was back at the Job Centre again. I had five or six jobs, one after the other. Nothing worked out. Nothing lasted. I had no money and I had no life.

But then I met a girl. We got on really well. I liked her a lot and I thought she felt the same. She used to say things like 'Money doesn't matter'. I began to believe her. But what happened? She ran off with her boss. He had a flash car. He was loaded.

It was then I began to go a bit crazy. I began to get ideas for making money that were not quite legal. And that's when I saw the advert that changed my life.

Time to take a break now.

Click off

It's hot in here. The sun is shining in at the window. That's one of the good things about living in Spain – plenty of sun. I think I'll have a cold beer. I won't eat anything yet. I'll wait for Maria to come in with that pizza.

3

That beer was good. Nice and cool. Let's carry on with the video. Now where was I? Oh yes – the day I saw that advert.

Click on

That advert was my start in life. It really was. That's what put me on the road to sunny Spain and good living. The old blood starts pumping when I think about the day I saw that advert.

I'd been hanging about in the street. Walking round and round. Going nowhere. A car came by – a silver Mercedes. The latest model. It hit a puddle and a jet of muddy water went all over me. I was wet from head to foot. And who was inside? I bet you can guess. It was my ex and her new boyfriend. They were laughing at me.

I felt hot with rage. The whole world seemed to go red. I began to run. I didn't care where I was going. Suddenly I found myself outside the Job Centre. And there in the window was the advert. WANTED. SECURITY VAN DRIVER. MUST HAVE CLEAN LICENCE.

I stared at the card in the window. Somehow I knew this job was my passport to money. Big money. I felt as if I'd been drowning. Now I was saved. The Devil had thrown me a line.

I got the job with Keepsafe Security and started the next Monday. They gave me a uniform with KEEPSAFE SECURITY on the jacket. I had a money bag and a chain to clip it to my arm. They gave me goggles in case some nutter tried to go for my eyes.

The boss told me what I had to do. By the end of the morning he reckoned I was trained up. I went round the back to pick up the van and meet the guy I'd be working with. His name was Joe. I could tell we were going to get along well. We hit it off right from the start.

The van was made like a tank. It had dark glass in the windows so nobody could see in. It looked evil. It had KEEPSAFE SECURITY in big yellow letters down the side. There was a safe for money inside. It looked as if it would take an army to blow it up.

Joe and I had to go and collect money from all the shops and stores. A few thousand here. A few thousand there. It all went into the safe in our van – thousands and thousands of pounds. We had to take the money to the bank. And we had to pick up money from the banks to pay workers in the factories.

We were like a ferry. But instead of people and cars we carried lots of lovely money. Money that was going to make a poor man rich. And I was the poor man. But not for much longer. I was on the way up. One day everyone would look up to me.

Click off

I'll stop for a bit. Where has Maria got to with my pizza? I bet she's chatting with her friends. Back in England everyone is in a hurry. But here in Spain they stand in the sun and chat to their friends. We all need friends, don't we? My mate Joe was a good friend. Where would I be now without poor old Joe?

4

Time to go on with my video. Time to tell you about Joe.

Click on

Joe knew the town. I drove the van, and he knew where to go and what stops to make. He knew the one-way streets and all the stores. He'd done the job for two years. When Joe told me to stop the van, I stopped. When we got the money in, we moved off again.

Everyone trusted Joe. He showed his pass and they handed over the cash. He put it in his bag and took it to the van safe. Then we moved on to the next place. I did the driving and Joe did the carrying. There was nothing to it.

Joe had been a policeman. He hated crooks. He would never take a penny that didn't belong to him. He was the right man for the job. He was a really nice guy. That's what I found hard to handle. There was a sort of red madness inside me and I had to hide it. I had to chat away to Joe as if laid back was my middle name.

To tell the truth it was driving me crazy. I was handling money every day of my life. It was like locking a kid in a chocolate factory and telling him to eat cabbage. I had to have a plan to make me rich. A good plan.

A good plan takes time. You must wait. You have to watch everything that happens. You have to carry on as normal. Your face must be a mask. If you rush into things you can end up inside for years.

The Devil had thrown me a life-line, but I had to keep calm. I wanted to do a one-off job. Make one big hit and win the jackpot. There had to be a way. And I'd find it as long as I didn't rush.

I had to be like the guy who called himself The Jackal. You know who I mean? You should know. The Jackal is famous. There are films about him. He tried to bump off the President of France.

Police all over the world were looking for The Jackal, but he ran rings round them. They couldn't even find out his real name. Did they get him in the end? They got someone, but was it The Jackal? No one can be sure.

The Jackal was big time. How did he do it? I'll tell you. He was super cool. He planned everything before he made a move. The Jackal was always in control.

But I wasn't The Jackal. I was just Jack. I had to be cool, or the Devil's life-line would drag me to hell. I had to start planning to get my hands on the money, money, money.

Click off

I'll stop for a bit. I bet Maria has forgotten all about my pizza. I eat too much, but so what? If I fancy something, I have it. I'm not just talking about food. Money gets you anything you want. And I don't like waiting for it.

5

Let's get the video going again. Ready.

Click on

My problem was always the same. I had to do things now. Right away. I could never wait. Waiting for anything drove me up the wall.

Wanting the money was driving me crazy. I felt like grabbing the money-bag from Joe, and running off with it. I had to make myself see sense. I'd be caught in two minutes flat. And for what? A few grand. There was no way I was going to prison for just one bag of money.

I needed something to calm me down. The doctor gave me some pills. They helped a bit. I got a note book and pen and put down my ideas. I tried to write out all the problems and think of ways to deal with them.

Where would I do the robbery? Where would I keep all that cash? Not under the bed . . . you need to put money in the bank, or you get no interest. A car costs £12,000 one year and £15,000 the next. See what I mean? Prices go up, so you need to make your money grow.

But if I put the money in the bank the police would soon be on to me. A big robbery would be in all the papers and on TV. Everyone would be after me. First trip to the bank and they'd nab me.

If only I could vanish when the job was done. Get rid of Jack and pop up as another person. I needed a new name. I needed a new identity.

But how could I turn into another person? What about the forms to be filled in? I'd need a passport . . . driving licence . . . NI number . . . all that stuff. I tried to be like The Jackal. I tried to plan every step. It was like a jigsaw. But the bits of the plan didn't fit.

I took more pills, and I began to drink. I couldn't sleep and I couldn't eat. I kept trying to finish my plan. I was making myself ill. My eyes were red and my hands were shaking.

Suddenly I snapped. I'd do it now. Right away. If I ended up inside, so what? It was better than going mad. If I got my hands on the money, I'd be OK. Pills were no good. Money was the drug I needed.

Click off

I have to stop the video. I'm shaking all over. It happens sometimes . . . when I think back . . . when I remember the past. I shake and shiver like a jelly. Did The Jackal ever feel like this? Did he shiver and feel sick? If he did, it wasn't in the film.

No need for Maria to hurry with that pizza. I'm not hungry now.

6

I feel OK now. I've stopped shaking. I'll get on with my story.

Click on

From now on it was go, go, go. Nothing was going to stop me. I got started. What did I do first? I rented a barn.

An old farmer had the barn. It was up on the moors –
not far from where I lived. I told the farmer I was
going to do up cars for sale. He lived on his own in an
old farmhouse. He didn't care what I did as long as I
paid him rent.

He had an old sheep truck in the yard. He hardly ever
used it, so I asked him if I could hire it. I said I
needed to pick up car parts. He wasn't too keen at
first, but I got him to change his mind for £50.

After the truck, I needed to get hold of someone's
passport. He had to be about my age. That's when I
had a stroke of luck. I heard one of the men at work
say he was going to Scotland for a holiday. He often
went abroad for holidays, and he said it would be a
nice change to stay in the UK.

It was just what I needed. He had a passport, and he
would leave it at home. I offered to keep an eye on his
house, and he gave me a key. The minute his car was
out of sight I was in his house. I was looking all over
the place for his passport. It only took me an hour to
find it.

He was the right age, and his hair was brown like
mine. But he had a beard. That was all right. I could
get a beard. Nothing to it. By the time he found out
his passport was gone, I'd be far away.

There was other stuff I had to get, and I had to work quickly. All the time my mind was full of lovely money. Big heaps of money that would soon be mine. The day I'd fixed was getting closer and closer.

Click off

7

Get a drink. Another beer. Be quick. Right. Now tell the camera about the big day. The day I got rich.

Click on

On the big day, Joe was already down at Keepsafe Security when I got there. He was having a cup of tea with a mate. He was saying, 'I've never been to a dentist in my life. I've never needed a dentist.' He looked up and grinned at me. I could see his lovely, white teeth.

I didn't smile back. I was shaking inside. Today was the day. Sink or swim, I had to go for it. It was now or never. 'Come on Joe. It's time to go,' I said.

'Just coming,' said Joe. 'You look a bit wild today, Jack. Didn't you get much sleep? If you like, I'll drive for a bit and you can have a little nap.'

That was the last thing I wanted. I'd been awake all night, but I had to drive. I didn't want Joe being nice to me. 'Shut up,' I said.

We got into the van and set off on the rounds. I crashed the gears. Joe told me to go steady. My foot was down. 'Take your time,' Joe said. 'Where's the fire?'

I made myself slow down. Joe was singing to himself. Out he got with his money-bag. Back came the money to the safe. Shops . . . stores . . . pubs . . . supermarkets. All the time the money was pouring in. We went to banks and picked up the wages. More money went in the safe.

I tried to be cool like The Jackal but I couldn't. I was burning up inside. I was driving through a red mist. That's how we went on all day. Until there was just one call to make. Just one more call.

It was a big factory. I had to drive into the yard while Joe went to the office right over the other side. It would take him twenty minutes to get back and by then I would be gone with the van and the money.

I drove into the yard and parked. Joe stared at my face. 'You look ill,' he said. 'Let me drive you home. We can do this job tomorrow.' Was Joe going to mess things up? If he didn't get out of the van, I'd have to hit him and throw him out.

My heart was beating like a hammer. My hands were wet with sweat. Somehow I put a smile on my face and said, 'I'm OK.' At last Joe put on his goggles. He got out of the van and walked away.

Now. It was now, now, now. I started the engine and put my foot to the floor.

As I drove along the road I felt as if everyone was looking at me. I wanted to get away fast but there was a lot of traffic. Very slow traffic. I kept saying, 'Come on, come on.' But I could only crawl along. My heart was knocking a hole in my chest.

At last I got to the street I wanted. It was run-down. Half the houses were empty. As I passed a slaughterhouse, I could hear the sound of cows and sheep. I sped down the street towards a little alley at the bottom. This is where I'd parked the farmer's sheep-truck.

Was it still there? I'd parked it first thing that morning, before it was light. Yes, it was there. I stopped the van just behind it and got out. I undid the back of the truck. Then I got into the Keepsafe Security van and drove it right inside the sheep-truck.

When I shut the back of the truck, no one could see the van hidden inside it.

I'd left an old jacket and cap under the driver's seat of the truck. I got in and put them on. They would hide my uniform.

I was trying to look like a farmer. A farmer who had just taken his sheep to the slaughterhouse. A farmer on his way home with an empty truck. Maybe I still looked like a robber with a van full of money hidden in his truck. So what? I was rich.

I got to the lights. Come on, come on. Change, change. I was going crazy. I hit my chest with my fist. The line of cars in front of me began to creep forward. 'Get out of my way!' I yelled. 'GET OUT OF MY WAY!'

Click off

Maria is here at last. She heard me shouting when she came in. She thought I was shouting at myself. 'No shout,' she said. That's how she talks. Her English isn't very good. 'No shout. No get upset. Here is pizza.'

9

*This is just what I need. A drink to steady my nerves,
and a pizza from the take-away next to the video shop.
They do the best pizzas. That reminds me – I told
Maria to take back that video I borrowed. It's overdue.
It's one of The Jackal films. The one called* The Day of
The Jackal. *She didn't take it back. I can see it on the
table over there.*

*Now, take a nice big bite of pizza. What's this? It's
ham – I hate ham. 'Maria, Maria, come here. Why
don't you do what I tell you? I told you to get
mushroom pizza. And you forgot to take that video
back. Put the pizza in the bin and get out. Go on.'*

*She's gone. But she'll soon be back. I often tell Maria
to get lost. She's used to it. I'd better carry on with my
video. Where was I? Oh yes, I was in the sheep-truck.*

Click on

When I was out of the town I began the long drive up
to the moors. The sheep-truck was old and slow. I got
to the farm at last and drove the truck into the barn I'd
rented.

First I had to get rid of my Keepsafe Security uniform.
I made a fire and soon the uniform was just a pile of

ash. I felt as if I'd burnt my old life. There was no going back now.

One thing I did know about was welding. I'd got a blowtorch. It was second-hand but it worked. I lit it and turned the gas up. The jet of flame hissed.

I stepped up into the back of the sheep-truck. There wasn't much room for me to work. The Keepsafe Security van filled most of the space. I pulled my welding helmet down and pointed the flame at the van. It was locked, and Joe had the key. But I didn't need a key.

The flame bit into the side of the van, like cutting butter. That was easy. The hard part was next – the safe.

It took me an hour to cut open the safe. And there inside was all that lovely money. The safe was crammed with it. £20 notes . . . £50 notes. There were even £100 notes.

I began to laugh. I couldn't help it. I laughed and laughed until the tears ran down my cheeks. Soon I would be on TV and in the papers. People would be saying 'Fancy him doing that. He seemed such a nice guy.'

I wiped my eyes. By now Joe would be at the police station. They'd be grilling him, and he wouldn't know what to say. He couldn't tell them anything because he didn't know anything. Poor old Joe. I began to laugh again. Then I felt like crying. I shut my eyes and tried to keep cool. Cool and calm like The Jackal.

What do you think of my plan so far? It was only half a plan, but it was good. It was working.

10

My barn was in the middle of nowhere. No one knew about it – no one except the farmer it belonged to. But if the robbery was on TV the farmer would see it. He knew me and he knew where I was. I had to move fast. I had to get to him before the news came on TV.

I ran over to the farmhouse. The light was on in the kitchen. I put my face to the window. I could see the farmer drinking a cup of tea and watching TV. The news was just coming on. I banged on the door. My heart was beating fast. Would the next part of my plan work?

When the farmer opened the door I held out a £50 note. I smiled and said, 'I know the rent isn't due yet but I'd like to pay now. Can I come in?' The money did the trick. He was all smiles. 'Come in. Sit down. Have a cup of tea.'

The rest was easy. I put sleeping pills in his tea – a lot of sleeping pills. Soon his head was on the kitchen table and he was snoring. He would be in the land of dreams for hours.

The TV was still on, but the farmer had missed the best bit of the news. A security van full of money had been stolen – two million pounds. The police were looking for the van and the driver.

They were looking for me, but I wasn't me any more. I had a passport to show I was someone else. And I wouldn't be driving a van – or a sheep-truck. No. I'd be driving a Range Rover. The farmer's Range Rover.

I hoped the keys for the Range Rover would be in the farmer's pocket, but they weren't. Where were they? I went into the hall. All his coats and jackets were hanging there. The keys were in a coat. Good – I'd got them. I turned off the TV and the lights. The farmer had a grandfather clock and it was tick-tocking in the darkness. It sent shivers up my spine.

I fell over a stool in my rush to get to the door. The farmer moved in his sleep and mumbled something. I froze. Was he waking up? No. He was snoring again. I dashed outside and bent over like a runner at the end of a race. My legs had gone to jelly.

Click off

Jelly. I'm hungry. I've got some jelly in the kitchen. My old Mum used to make jelly for me when I was a kid. Maria makes it the same way. Maybe that's why I like it. Funny, isn't it? I can afford to eat anything I want, and here I am eating jelly. Just like I did when I was a kid with no money.

11

Click on

Now that I'd fixed the farmer I had to put my money into his Range Rover. It didn't take long. I stuffed all the money into two big sacks and hid them under all the junk in the back.

I had to hurry. It was almost midnight and there was one more thing for me to do. Something to keep the police off my track for a bit longer.

I went back to the barn and got the sheep-truck. I drove it down a path that led to a cliff. There was a lake at the bottom – a deep lake.

The moon was bright so I didn't need to put the lights on. The truck bumped up and down over ruts on the path. I could hear bits of the Keepsafe Security van and the broken safe banging about in the back.

I drove to the edge of the cliff and jumped out as the truck was still moving. It went right over. I saw it crash into the water. Then I saw it bob up again. No, no . . . it had to sink. It had to go under. Yes, at last it was sinking. The water sucked it down. The truck, the van, the safe, everything – it was all gone.

I ran back to get the Range Rover. The moon was behind a cloud. I could hardly see where I was going. I kept falling over ruts, and running into bushes.

At last I got back to the Range Rover. I checked my money just to make sure it was still there. I put my arm right inside one of the sacks and let my fingers play with the crisp notes. Then I turned the key and I was away. Soon I was belting down the M1 with two million pounds on the back seat.

Click off

What a moment that was. I was rich and I felt as free as a bird. Telling my story is making me re-live it all . . . the bad bits and the good bits. I'm getting a real buzz from the good bits.

12

I think I'll have a quick shave and brush my hair. I want to look good for the camera. I could put on a silk shirt – the one that cost about £500. Why didn't I put it on before I started? Never mind. I'll put it on now.

Right, I'm ready. I look good.

Click on

Down the M1 I went in the Range Rover. It was still dark but not for much longer. Would I be out of England before the sun came up? I turned onto the M25 and headed for the Channel Tunnel.

The M25. You know what that's like, don't you? They call it the world's longest car-park. Not the place to go if you are in a hurry. But it's not so bad at night.

I went flying down the fast lane like a bat out of hell. I was way over the speed limit. I knew I was taking a risk but I felt lucky. Then I saw the blue light in my mirror – the flashing blue light. A police car.

I was only a few miles from the Channel Tunnel. It crossed my mind to make a dash for it but what was the use? Even if I shook this lot off my tail, their mates would be waiting for me down the road.

I slowed down and stopped on the hard shoulder. When the police walked up to me, my mouth went dry. 'Is this your car, Sir?' I opened my mouth but I didn't know what to say.

Suddenly a cattle truck went past. Like magic the cops all ran to their car. They left me standing there. They didn't even look back at me. Then the siren was going, the blue light was flashing and they were off after the truck.

Why? I'll tell you why. They must have got a tip-off about my cattle truck. Now they were after every cattle truck in the country. I started the Range Rover and drove on – not too fast, not too slow.

Two miles down the road the cattle truck had stopped. There were police cars all round it. Up in the air there was a helicopter. As I went by I heard all the cows in the truck mooing. I found myself laughing. I laughed until the tears ran down my cheeks.

I was still laughing when I got to the Tunnel. In my pocket I'd got a fake beard to make me look like the photo in my stolen passport. How's that for planning?

Does that make you think of The Jackal? He kept changing the way he looked.

But I wasn't The Jackal. The beard was rubbish. It made me look like someone in a Christmas panto. I put it back in my pocket. If anyone asked about my beard, I'd say I shaved it off.

No one asked. They hardly bothered to look at my stolen passport. Ten minutes later I was in the Tunnel heading for France.

Click off

13

I can see Maria in the garden. She's thinking about coming in but she's afraid I'll shout at her again. I'll call to her. 'Maria, Maria. I'm busy now, but later on you can tidy up in here and cook me a meal. Stay out there until I call you.'

Click on

It was morning and the sun was shining. There I was driving along the French motorway. I was free and all around me I could see fields and trees and blue sky. Does that sound good?

It wasn't good. I was tired. I was hungry. And the Range Rover was running out of fuel. I had two million pounds on the back seat but it was English money. It was no use in France.

Why not go to a bank and change the money? I'll tell you why. The farmer would be awake by now. The police would know that I'd rented his barn and stolen his Range Rover. They'd put two and two together. The missing two million pounds . . . the missing Range Rover.

They could be on to me right now. Right now. The French police would be looking for an English man in a Range Rover. They would have the number. I had to get rid of the Range Rover. I had to get it off the road. I turned off the motorway, and soon I was driving along country lanes.

I kept going until I was on the edge of a forest. Just the place to dump the car. But I needed to get right into the trees. Here and there I saw little paths that went into the forest. Most of them were too small for the Range Rover, but one was a bit bigger – a kind of forest track. Right. This was the one for me.

I drove deep into the trees. Then I stopped the car and opened up the back. I pulled the sacks of money out from under all the junk. I peeped inside to make sure the money was still there. Maybe all of this was just a crazy dream. No, it was real. I could see the money.

I found a hole in a tree and put the sacks inside. Then I covered the hole with grass and twigs. I went to the Range Rover and let the handbrake off. I pushed it into the bushes. I kept pushing. There was a slope. The car began to roll. Down it went – deep into the tall weeds and ferns. No one would see it now.

What was I going to do next? I needed a car and I needed food. How could I get them? My legs felt weak so I sat down. The ground was wet and muddy but I didn't care. I was dead tired. I lay on my back under the bushes. In no time I was asleep.

14

I woke up with a jump. What was that? I could hear a gun. There it was again – and again. Gunshots. It must be the police coming to get me. This was the end.

Then I stopped to think. The gunshots were far away in the forest. Lots of French people like to hunt. They go out and shoot birds. That's what I could hear. It was just a hunter out for a bit of sport.

Was my money still OK? I ran back to the tree where it was hidden. I got a shock. There was a car – a small blue car. A Renault. It was parked just a few steps away from my money. The hunter must have left it here when I was asleep. He could have put it next to any tree in the forest but he picked this one.

What a shock. But what a bit of luck. I needed a car and here it was. The hunter had left the windows wide open and the keys were inside. It was too good to be true.

On the back seat was a paper bag. I grabbed it and looked inside. Some cheese, some bread and a big lump of cooked meat. A packed lunch for a hunter. I stuffed the cheese in my mouth.

That's when I heard the dog. A dog was barking. It was loud. It was close. And it was getting closer. It must be the hunter's dog. I took a step towards the car. I could jump in and drive away, but what about my money? Maybe I could . . . no. It was too late. The dog came dashing out of the bushes.

It was a big dog. The kind that can rip you to bits. When it saw me it froze for a moment. I was a stranger standing by the master's car. And I was eating the master's food. The dog went mad. It ran at me like a rocket.

Big teeth snapped at my arm. Rip went my jacket, rip went my shirt. How could I get away? The tree. I had to go up the tree. I tried to grab a branch but it was too high. Then I put my foot inside the tree trunk. I used the sacks of money as a step. Up into the branches I went.

The dog was going crazy at the bottom of the tree. It was jumping up and barking. Suddenly I heard a man calling out in French. The hunter was coming after his dog.

Now the dog was sniffing at my money. I saw it grab the end of a sack and tug at it. I began to panic. I almost fell out of the tree. I was shaking so much that I dropped the paper bag full of food.

That bag of food saved me. As soon as it hit the ground the dog jumped on it. When the hunter came running up to the tree he saw his dog eating his packed lunch. He was hopping mad. The hunter was so busy hitting his dog that he didn't see me up in the tree. And he didn't see the sack of money sticking out of the tree trunk.

Soon he walked away into the forest. He was keen to get on with the day's sport. The dog trotted behind him with its tail between its legs. It looked back and gave one last bark, but I was safe. That dog wasn't going to run away from its master again.

A few minutes later I loaded my sacks of money into the blue Renault, and I was on my way. No need to worry about petrol. The tank was almost full. Sunny Spain here I come.

Click off

I think I'll move the camera a bit. Just a little bit. I want my face to be nice and clear in the video. I was a bit shy when I started telling my story, but I'm getting the hang of it now.

15

This is going to be a good video. It's a pity that I can't show it to anyone. I'll get it finished today and tomorrow I must put it in my strong-box at the bank. It will stay there for the rest of my life. My secret. My true life story.

Click on

I drove the blue Renault back to the motorway, and then I really put my foot down. I was dreaming of Spain, but I wasn't there yet. I kept telling myself that everything would be OK when I got to Spain.

Soon it began to get dark. Another day was almost over. I put the headlights on and the road signs shone in the darkness. I watched them flash by. Spain was getting closer and closer. I'd be at the border in half an hour.

Suddenly I jumped. Where was I? I was still racing down the fast lane, but I'd been asleep. Just for a few seconds my eyes had been shut. I almost hit another car. My eyes were open now and I was shaking all over.

There was a turning off the motorway and I took it. I stopped right there and got out of the car. My legs were so stiff I almost fell over. I rubbed them and looked back at the motorway. It was like a great river of light in the darkness.

A police car went speeding by. Then another – and another. A pack of police cars. They were all going flat out down the motorway to Spain. I had to smile. Here I was and they had gone right past me.

I didn't smile for long. If I went back to the motorway the police would be waiting for me at the border. I had to find another way to cross to Spain.

There are mountains all along the border between France and Spain. The police could block all the main roads but they couldn't block every little track and path. Could I find a track that went over the mountains?

If I had a map I could do it. But what about petrol? The tank was almost empty. I stood there telling myself how stupid I was. I wanted to be like The Jackal but I had set off without a proper plan. Now what could I do?

I had to keep cool. There must be a map of some kind in the car. Everyone keeps a map in the car. I was right. I found plenty of maps. Maps of France. Maps of Spain. And that's not all – I found two cans of petrol, a big bottle of water and a bag of sweets. Great!

After a good look at the maps I was on my way again. I drove along little roads in the darkness. At first I saw a few signposts, but after that I had to guess which way to go. The road kept turning. I went round bend after bend. And all the time I was going uphill. Up and up.

I knew that I must be right up in the mountains by now, but it was too dark to see them. All round me there was thick darkness. My headlights lit up a little bit of track in front of me. That's all I could see as I drove on. Just a little bit of track which kept bending and turning. Up and up. Round and round. Up and up.

I was tired and cold. I needed to sleep. Fear had kept me going, but now sleep was pressing down on my eyelids. Soon I would stop for a rest. Soon I would sleep . . . sleep . . . sleep. A tree. A tree coming at me. Turn the wheel. Where's the track? CRASH! Everything went black.

Click off

I'll stop for a minute.

16

That crash was almost the end of me. I get upset just thinking about it. Never mind, I'm safe now. I'm here in my nice villa. Maria is out there by the pool. Everything is OK.

Click on

I opened my eyes. My nose was bleeding and there were cuts all over my arms. The car windscreen was just broken glass. I had crashed into a tree, and branches were sticking right into the car.

I dragged myself out into the night. The air was icy cold. There was a funny glow coming from the ground. It was snow. I was up so high that I was in the snow zone.

What now? What next? I told myself not to panic. I would sleep until the sun came up. When it was light I could have a good look at the car. I needed to keep warm. It would be easy to freeze to death up here.

I had an idea. I pulled my sacks of money out of the smashed car. Money is made of paper. Paper would keep the cold out. I opened a sack and got right into it. It was like a sleeping bag – a sleeping bag stuffed with money.

Anything could happen to me now. A wolf might creep up on me. Yes, there are wolves in the mountains of Spain. At last I fell asleep.

When I opened my eyes the sun was shining. For a minute I didn't know where I was. Then I looked round. What I saw took my breath away. All round me there were mountain peaks. Snow glittered in the sunshine. I was on top of the world.

What about the car? It was hanging on the side of the mountain. Under it there was a great drop. A tree was holding the car up. The tree was stopping it from falling down, down, down into a deep valley. I felt dizzy just looking at the drop. Last night I was sitting in that car – hanging in the air. I tried to put the thought out of my mind.

The car was no use so I got the sacks onto my back and began to walk. I tried to plan as I plodded along. I needed to get out of these mountains and go to a bank. I had to change my money and use that stolen passport before the owner got back from his holiday in Scotland. I smiled as I thought about the mountains of Scotland. They would look like little hills if you put them next to the mountains all around me.

It's hard to remember the next part of my story. I got so hungry and worn out that it's all a blur in my mind. I know that I walked for miles. The sacks of money made me feel like a donkey with a heavy load on its back. Then I found a real donkey and rode it until I was out of the mountains. I remember that I dug up some carrots and potatoes in a field and ate them raw. When I got to a little village I stole an old van.

Somehow I kept going. I kept pressing on.

17

At last I had crossed Spain and I was on the coast. There was the sea. Miles and miles of bright blue sea . . . yellow sand . . . people on holiday, swimming. The time had come to go to a bank and change my money. If I didn't hurry up and change it I might as well throw it into the sea.

Would my stolen passport work? Would it fool a bank? The photo showed a man with a beard. My beard had grown so that was OK. But what about the rest of me?

My clothes were torn and dirty. I hadn't washed for days and I smelt like the inside of a rubbish bin. And what would they think if I went into a bank dragging my money in two old sacks? I locked the money in the van and went on to the beach.

I went for a long swim in the warm, blue sea. I splashed about with all the holiday-makers but I kept an eye on the beach. I swam along until I saw what I wanted. A big backpack all by itself on the sand.

In a flash I was out of the water and that backpack was mine. The owner would have a problem when he came back from his swim. I'd got all his clothes. They were in the backpack.

The nearest big city was Barcelona. That's where I went. I dumped the old van and soon I was just one of the crowd. Just another English guy on holiday with a smile on his face, a T-shirt and shorts that didn't fit very well – and a big, heavy backpack. Now I was ready to go to a bank.

I needed to change my money fast. But if I changed too much at one go they would be on to me. I had to hold back. I had to change a bit here and a bit there. Right. Go for it.

As I stood in the bank my heart was thudding like a drum. I thought everyone would hear it. But it was OK. I showed my stolen passport. I handed over £200. They changed it for me. It was easy. It all went like a dream.

Now that I had a bit of cash, I got a room at a small hotel. Then I set off to change more money. Soon the stolen passport would be no good to me. Any day now the owner would report it missing. It was a race against time.

I dashed from bank to bank and I went to a few big hotels where they change money. I never changed more than £200 at one go. At the end of three days I had changed about £10,000. Not bad. It would keep me going for now. After that I burnt the passport. It would be my passport to jail if I kept on using it.

You might think that everything was OK now. But it wasn't. The good life was still out of reach. All the time I worried about money. How could I change the rest of my English pounds? And how could I keep my money safe?

The bank is the place for money. But I had to keep mine in my room or carry it around with me. You can't have much fun with a heavy pack dragging you down. I felt like a snail with a big shell on my back – a shell of money. But if I let it out of my sight someone might steal it.

Click off

I'll get another beer. No I won't. I don't want to get drunk before this video is finished. I drink too much. I get drunk when I feel lonely. And I miss Joe. My mate Joe. I wish he was here with me now. I'll have that drink after all.

18

Click on

Days went by. Weeks went by. Most of the time I stayed in my room keeping an eye on my cash. I kept counting it to pass the time. A big pile of English money and a small pile of money I could spend. Sometimes I went down to a little bar close to the hotel. I sat there with a glass of wine and read the English paper. But I couldn't relax. I kept dashing back to my room to make sure my money was safe.

Do you see what had happened to me? I was a slave to my money. I'd come all this way to be free and I was like a prisoner.

Then one day something happened. I was sitting in the little bar near the hotel and someone tapped me on the back. I jumped and turned round. It was Joe. 'Hello Jack,' he said. 'I knew it was you. It takes more than a beard to fool an ex-policeman.'

I just stared at him. I felt as if the floor had opened up under me. 'How did you find me?' I asked. Joe looked surprised and said, 'I didn't come to Spain to find you Jack. I came here to start a new life.'

I tried to make sense of what he was saying. If he hadn't come to track me down, why was he here? Joe got himself a drink and sat down. 'You messed up my life Jack,' he said. 'They thought I was mixed up in the robbery. They couldn't prove anything but they gave me the sack. No one trusts me now. That's what you did to me, Jack. You took away my good name.'

Joe's face was sad and old as he sipped his drink. He said, 'There was nothing to keep me in England. No family. No ties. No future. So I put my savings into a Spanish bank and here I am.'

In a funny way Joe was in the same boat as me. We both needed a new life and now fate had brought us together. Me and my old mate Joe. Suddenly I could see my future opening up in front of me. Joe wasn't on the run like me. He could help me. And then we could both live the good life.

'Where are you staying?' I asked. Joe pointed to a car parked outside the bar. 'See that car? All my stuff is in there. I've just bought myself a little flat and I was on my way to move in. I haven't seen the place yet but it's mine.' He took the keys of the flat from his pocket and put them on the table.

'I'll come with you,' I said. 'You don't know how lonely I've been. But now it will be like old times. I'll make you rich, Joe. We can use your bank account and I'll split my money with you. Fifty-fifty. We'll be partners. You lost your job because of me but I'll make it up to you.'

'Yes, Jack, you will make it up to me,' said Joe. His eyes were shining and all his sadness had gone. He picked up the keys to the flat and laughed. 'I won't need these after all,' he said. 'I'm going to hand you over to the law, Jack. I'm going to turn you in. Then I can hold up my head again and I can go home. I don't need a new life.'

I tried to talk him out of it but anyone would think he was still in the police. He said he had to do his duty. He had to do what was right. 'What about me?' I asked. 'I'm your old mate. Don't you care about me? How can you be so selfish?'

'I do care,' said Joe. 'But I've got to do this. You'll go to jail but it won't be for life, Jack. You took money – a lot of money. But you didn't hurt anyone. Robbery is a crime but it's not like murder.'

It was Joe who said the word murder, not me. He made me think of it. Suddenly everything clicked into place in my head. I had a plan. When I set off I had half a plan, but I didn't know how to end it. It was luck that got me this far. But now my plan was finished.

Joe thought he knew me. He thought I was just an ordinary chap. But I had changed. I was super cool. I was ready to follow my plan step by step. And I was ready to kill. I was like The Jackal.

Click off

19

I wish my video was a proper film. I'm telling my story but its not like a film where you can see all the action. Maybe someone will film it one day. Years from now when I'm dead and gone, my secret video will see the

light of day. It will make the world sit up. I think
someone will film it, don't you? Everyone likes a good
murder story.

Click on

Joe didn't know what was going on in my mind. My
brain was going click, click, click, like a computer
game. But I hid my thoughts from Joe. I played a
part.

'I'll go with you,' I said. 'I'll give myself up. You're
right Joe. It's the best thing to do. I've been unhappy
ever since I stole that money. Now I want to put
things right. I don't want to go on running.'

Joe patted me on the back like a father saying well
done to his kid. He believed me. He believed every
word I said. I pointed to my hotel across the road.
'We'd better go and get all the money. It's in my room.'

We went to my hotel. Joe followed me up the stairs
and into my little room. There was some cash on the
bed. I opened a cupboard and more money fell out.
My big backpack was standing in a corner. I undid
the zip and showed Joe all the money inside. There
was money everywhere.

'You didn't spend much,' said Joe. He was right. Most
of the two million was still there. I wanted to spend it.

I was dying to spend it. I got stuck because I didn't have a bank account or any ID. But I didn't tell Joe about that. Instead I stood looking at my feet and said, 'I want to give it all back.'

Joe nodded and said, 'That's good, Jack. It will help your case when you go to court. Now let's pack all this money up. We can put it in my car and drive to the nearest police station. The Spanish police will ring England.'

He began stuffing all the loose money into the backpack and I stood behind him. Very slowly I picked up my bedside lamp. The base was solid metal. Joe was chatting away about how he would help me. How I'd be out of prison in no time. He didn't see me lift the lamp high in the air.

There was a thump as the lamp hit the back of Joe's head. He fell face down on the bed. I told myself that he didn't feel it. How could he? It was over in a second.

Click off

I'll just stop and wipe my eyes. I'm not crying. Why should I cry about Joe? He made me kill him. We could have had fun with all my money. I just needed him to help me – be on my side. But he let me down.

20

My eyes are still watering. It happens a lot these days. Maybe I've got hayfever. I need to see the doctor about it.

Click on

Joe was lying on the bed very still. There wasn't much blood. Just a few drops running down behind his ear onto the bed cover. I got a towel and put it round his head.

I felt in one of Joe's pockets. Here were his car keys, and here were the keys to his flat. Now the next pocket. Good. I'd found his passport and his bankbook. In another pocket there was a big wallet with money in it and a lot of papers.

Now I could really start to live. I could use Joe's bank. I could move into his flat. I'd got all the ID I needed. I had everything to say I was Joe.

I left Joe on the bed and ran downstairs to pay my bill. I gave the man at the desk a big tip and said that I'd be leaving tonight. Maybe very late. No need to help me with my bags.

Joe's car was down the road. I got in and drove it right up to the door of my hotel. I packed my clothes and a few other things into the car. Then I had to wait. It would be easy to move my money . . . but everyone had to be out of the way when I moved Joe.

I sat in my room waiting for night to come. I kept looking at Joe's body. I tried to read a book but all the time I could see Joe's body out of the corner of my eye. Every now and then I thought I saw it move. But when I looked again it was still.

The sky got dark and the hours went slowly by. At last all the noise in the street stopped. It was time to go. I rolled Joe over. One eye was open and it seemed to be looking at me. Then suddenly the other eye popped open.

I gave a yell and jumped back. What could I do? A pillow. Yes. I grabbed a pillow and pressed it over his face. I felt sick. He had to be dead now.

I grabbed the bed cover and pulled it right round Joe's body. Then I got him onto my back. Joe was a big man but no bigger than me. I went down the stairs with Joe's legs bumping on each step. I was down. I was outside. The body was in the car.

I dashed back to get my money. The big backpack was heavy but after Joe it seemed light. A bedroom door opened as I went down the stairs, and a woman in a nightdress stared out at me. It was just as well she didn't open her door when I was carrying the body.

A moment later I was in the car and I was driving away.

Click off

I need to stand up and take a deep breath. I wasn't looking forward to that part of my story. It's the bit I can't get out of my mind. I dream about it every night. I see Joe's face. I know he's dead but his eyes are looking at me. Why do I keep dreaming about it?

21

Let's forget about my dreams and get on with the story.

Click on

I got out of Barcelona and drove for miles. I stopped at a place where the cliffs jut out over the sea. The stars were very bright. They were like little eyes looking at me. It was time to get rid of Joe.

First I rolled him out of the bloodstained cover. Then I took all his clothes off. I dragged his bare white body across the grass to the cliff. Then I pushed him over. He made a little splash as he hit the sea far below.

No one would ever know who he was. Even if the body got washed up they would never know. There would be nothing to go on. They would look at his teeth. Everyone has different teeth and dentists keep a record.

But Joe had no record. I told you about his teeth. Remember? They were perfect. Joe had never been to a dentist in his life.

Soon the stars faded and the sky began to get light. I got into Joe's car and set off to find Joe's flat – my flat. I'd got a passport, a bank-book and all the things I needed to start my new life. From now on I'd be Joe. I could see my face in the car mirror. I looked a lot like Joe. Not so old – but very like him. I felt like Joe already.

As I drove along I talked to my face in the mirror. 'Hello, I'm Joe. Just call me Joe. I've got a little flat but I'm going to buy myself a villa . . . with a swimming pool and a view of the sea. I'll need a maid to cook and clean for me. Who's Jack? Never heard of him. My name is Joe.'

Well, that's about it. You know the rest of my story. You know that my plan worked and I got all the things

I wanted. So here I am in my villa making this video. Everyone thinks I'm Joe. But you know the truth.

I did well, didn't I? Most people make mistakes. They mess things up – but not me. My plan was perfect. The Jackal himself never made a better plan.

Where did I put that video about The Jackal? Here it is. I'll hold it up so you can see the title. It's called *The Day Of The Jackal*. I've played it over and over again so I know it's a good story. But mine is better. I think it's much better. Telling my story has made me see myself as I really am. I'm a hero.

I didn't let fate push me around. I grabbed a lucky star and I made it shine down on me. And that's how it's going to be from now on. At the end of my long happy life my secret video will be found. Then I'll be famous. I'll take my place in history.

Right. I've finished. You can clap now. You can cheer if you like.

Click off

22

*I've done it . . . my own life story . . . my own video. I'd
better take it out of the recorder. That's it.*

*Now I feel really good. Better than I've felt for ages.
I've taken the past out of my head and put it on a video.
So I can lock it away and forget it, can't I? Tomorrow I'll
put it in my strong-box at the bank.*

*'Joe! Joe!' That's Maria calling. It still gives me a shock
when she calls me Joe. She's been waiting outside in
the garden for hours. I'll send her into town. She can
take that Jackal video back and buy some food. I fancy
a nice home-cooked meal later on.*

*I'm going to relax now. I'll have a swim then I'll sit by
the pool in the sunshine.*

* * * * * *

*Have I been out here for two hours? I must have fallen
asleep. I'll go in and see if my meal is ready. I'm
hungry. Mmmm it smells good. Why is this Jackal
video still sitting on the table?*

'Maria, come here. I told you to take The Day Of The
Jackal *back to the shop.'*

'Yes, Joe. I take it back.'

'Don't be silly. It's still here.'

'Maybe I make a mistake. A mix-up. Maybe I take another video in the Jackal packet.'

'Which video? Which video did you take?'

'Stop it, Joe. You hurt my arm. I find a video by the TV. I take it to the video shop and a man is asking for crime video. He take it out again right away.'

'Who was he? Stop crying and tell me. I've got to find him. I've got to get that video back.'

'I see him in the shop before. He is on holiday with his wife and kids. Always he take out crime video. He is a policeman.'

'I feel ill. I'm dizzy. Help me, Maria. There's a banging noise inside my head.'

'It's the door. Someone banging on the door.'

'Don't open it, Maria. Lock it. Lock it now!'

'Police are here, Joe. Lots of police. They ask for Jack. They say Jack is here. I tell them no – just me and Joe. But they smash the door. They have guns. Look out, Joe!'

53

The Spirals Series

Stories

Jim Alderson
Crash in the Jungle
The Witch Princess

Jan Carew
Death Comes to the Circus
Footprints in the Sand

Barbara Catchpole
Laura Called
Nick

Susan Duberley
The Ring

Keith Fletcher and Susan Duberley
Nightmare Lake

John Goodwin
Dead-end Job
Ghost Train

Paul Groves
Not that I'm Work-shy

Marian Iseard
Loved To Death

Anita Jackson
The Actor
The Austin Seven
Bennet Manor
Dreams
The Ear
A Game of Life or Death
No Rent to Pay

Paul Jennings
Eye of Evil
Maggot

Margaret Loxton
The Dark Shadow

Patrick Nobes
Ghost Writer

David Orme
City of the Roborgs
The Haunted Asteroids

Kevin Philbin
Summer of the Werewolf

Bill Ridgway
Jack's Video

Julie Taylor
Spiders

John Townsend
Back on the Prowl
Beware of the Morris Minor
Fame and Fortune
Night Beast
SOS
A Minute to Kill
Snow Beast

Plays

Jan Carew
Computer Killer
No Entry
Time Loop

Julia Donaldson
Books and Crooks

John Godfrey
When I Count to Three

Paul Groves
Tell Me Where it Hurts

Barbara Mitchelhill
Punchlines
The Ramsbottoms at Home

John Townsend
A Bit of a Shambles
A Lot of Old Codswallop
Breaking the Ice
Cheer and Groan
Clogging the Works
Cowboys, Jelly and Custard
Hanging by a Fred
The Lighthouse Keeper's Secret
Making a Splash
Over and Out
Rocking the Boat
Spilling the Beans
Taking the Plunge

David Walke
The Good, the Bad and the Bungle
Package Holiday